A recipe book by a true cookery nerd

By

Michael Thomsen

Copyright © 2017
All rights reserved

Introduction

Hello!

My name is Michael Thomsen.

I said in my last book that I can honestly not think of a more versatile and well-rounded meal than a burger, and by round I don't mean its shape. Pizza might just be it, and it's round too.

I am not a chef by any means, but I am very passionate about cooking. I have been grilling with my old man since I was a little boy and I am happy to have carried out this tradition with my children.

In this cookbook, you will find a collection of a variety of delicious pizza. Here are some of my favorite recipes to cook at home.
I hope you're hungry!

Table of content
The Mexi 4

The Mac & Cheese 6

The Bucket 8

The Stromboli 10

The First Meal Of The Day 12

The Cauliflower Special 14

The Feathery Crust 16

The Crust Is Always Greener On The Other Side 17

The Fake Italian 20

The Pinwheels 22

The Pizzadillas 24

The Time Garlic Bread Met Pizza 26

The Skillet 28

The Hot Pocket 30

The Ranch Pig 32

The Swiss 34

The Roll Out 36

The Pull-Apart Pizza 38

The Mexi

Ingredients

- 1 1/2 tbsp. extra-virgin olive oil
- Cooking spray
- 8 oz. lean ground beef
- 1 packet taco seasoning
- kosher salt
- Freshly ground black pepper
- 1 1/2 c. shredded cheddar, divided
- 1 12" flour tortilla
- 1 heaping cup shredded romaine
- 1/4 c. sour cream
- 1 diced roma tomato
- 1/2 avocado, thinly sliced

Instructions

Heat your oven to an even 400º. Spray a baking sheet lightly with a cooking oil of your choosing, we recommend olive oil. or use parchment paper.

Add your olive oil, seasoning, salt, pepper and meat in a small skillet until nice and cooked through.

Put your tortillas on your lightly oiled baking sheet and add half a cup of cheese. Top your tortilla with your meat and another half a cup of cheese and cook in the oven until melted, it should take around 5 minutes

Take it out of the oven and add the remaining cheese. Top the pizza with the rest of your ingredients and serve warm.

The Mac & Cheese

Ingredients

- 1 box macaroni and cheese, plus ingredients called for on box
- 1 c. shredded cheddar, divided
- 1 c. shredded mozzarella, divided
- 1 lb. pizza dough
- Extra-virgin olive oil, for brushing
- 1/4 tsp. garlic powder
- 1/4 tsp. Italian seasoning
- kosher salt
- Freshly ground black pepper
- Freshly chopped parsley, for serving

Instructions

Heat your oven to an even 400°. Spray a baking sheet lightly with a cooking oil of your choosing, we recommend olive oil. or use parchment paper.

Follow the instructions on the packing of the macaroni and cheese, add half cup cheddar and half cup mozzarella to a small pot. mix it till well combined.

Roll out the pizza dough into a large regular pizza side and place on the baking sheet/parchment paper. Dip cooking brush in olive oil and evenly brush the dough and season with the powdered garlic. put in the oven and let it cook until golden brown, should take around 10 minutes.

Top with the macaroni and cheese and add the remaining cheese. bake again until the newly added cheese is melted.

Sprinkle with the parsley and serve warm.

The Bucket

Ingredients

- 1 8-oz. tube crescent dough
- 1/4 c. pizza sauce
- 1 c. shredded mozzarella
- 1/2 c. freshly grated Parmesan
- 1 c. large pepperoni slices
- 1 tsp. Italian seasoning

Instructions

Heat your oven to an even 400°. Spray a muffin tin lightly with a cooking oil of your choosing, we recommend olive oil. or use parchment paper.

Flour your kitchen counter and unroll the crescent dough and separate it to four equally sized rectangles.

Slice your dough in half lengthwise. Spoon out a thin layer of pizza sauce on each piece of dough. Top with cheese, pepperoni. make sure the pepperoni slightly overlap and make sure half of each of them is off the dough. Finish off with another slice of dough and roll them up so the look like roses.

Place each pizza rose in the greased muffin tin and bake for around 20 min or until golden brown.

Serve warm.

The Stromboli

Ingredients

- 1 lb. pizza dough, at room temperature
- ½ c. pizza sauce
- 4 slices ham
- 24 slices pepperoni
- 2 oz. cremini mushrooms, thinly sliced
- ½ Green Bell Pepper, chopped
- 1 c. shredded mozzarella
- 1 egg, beaten
- 1 tbsp. freshly grated Parmesan
- ½ tsp. Italian seasoning

Instructions

Heat your oven to an even 400º. Spray baking sheet lightly with a cooking oil of your choosing, we recommend olive oil. or use parchment paper.

Roll out the pizza dough into a large regular pizza side and place on the baking sheet/parchment paper. Spoon out pizza sauce evenly, leaving half an inch of the edge of the dough.

Top with the meats, peppers and mushroom. Drizzle the mozzarella cheese and brush the edges with egg or olive oil.

Carefully roll the dough like a cinnamon roll, seal the edges shut. Brush all over with egg or olive oil. season with Italian seasoning and sprinkle with parmesan cheese.

Bake until golden brown, it should take 30 minutes. Take it out of the oven and let it set for 10 minutes.

Slice and serve.

The First Meal Of The Day

Ingredients

- 1 lb. store-bought pizza dough, thawed if frozen
- 1 tbsp. extra-virgin olive oil, plus more for greasing pan
- 2 c. shredded mozzarella
- 1 c. diced ham
- 5 large eggs
- Freshly ground black pepper
- Fresh parsley, for garnish

Instructions

Heat your oven to an even 400º. Spray a baking sheet lightly with a cooking oil of your choosing, we recommend olive oil. or use parchment paper. Sprinkle mozzarella and ham. Crack five eggs on top and season with pepper.

Bake the pizza until golden, make sure the eggs is still soft. Garnish with parsley and serve.

The Cauliflower Special

Ingredients

- 1 large head cauliflower, roughly chopped and steamed
- 1 large egg
- 2 c. shredded mozzarella, divided
- 1/2 c. freshly grated Parmesan, divided
- Zest from 1/2 lemon
- kosher salt
- Freshly ground black pepper
- 1/4 c. Alfredo Sauce
- 1 clove garlic, thinly sliced
- 1/4 c. red onion, thinly sliced
- 1/4 c. cherry tomatoes, halved
- 1 small zucchini, shaved into a few lengthwise ribbons
- Torn fresh basil, for garnish

Instructions

Preheat oven to 425°.

Pulse your steamed cauliflower in a food processor until it has a grated-like texture. use a cheesecloth or dish towel and squeeze out the water.

In a large mixing bowl transfer cauliflower and the egg, half of the mozzarella, half of the parmesan and zest lemon. Season well with salt and pepper.

Spray a baking sheet lightly with a cooking oil of your choosing, we recommend olive oil. or use parchment paper. Add your dough and spread it out into a thin crust. Bake the dough until dry, it should take around 15-20 minutes.

Top with Alfredo Sauce, garlic, remaining cheeses and the vegetables. Bake your assembled pizza, the cheese should be melted and the crust nice and crispy after 10-12 minutes. Take it out and spread basil all over the pizza.

The Feathery Crust

Ingredients

- 1 lb. ground chicken
- 1 1/2 c. shredded mozzarella
- 1 tsp. garlic powder
- kosher salt
- Freshly ground black pepper
- 1/4 c. barbecue sauce
- 1 c. shredded gouda
- 1/3 c. sliced red onion
- 2 tbsp. Sliced green onions
- Ranch, for drizzling

Instructions

Heat your oven to an even 400º. Spray a baking sheet lightly with a cooking oil.

Combine minced chicken a third of the mozzarella, powdered garlic and season with salt and pepper.

Using the chicken mixture create the pizza "crusts".

Put the chicken in the oven and cook it until well done.

Spoon out a layer of bbq sauce on the chicken crust and top with guada and the rest of the mozzarella. drizzle with more bbq sauce and top with the onions.

Using the broil setting until the cheese melted. Spread ranch dressing and serve right away!

The Crust Is Always Greener On The Other Side

Ingredients

- 1 large head broccoli, chopped and steamed
- 1 large egg
- 2 c. shredded mozzarella, divided
- 1/2 c. Parmesan, divided
- 1/2 tsp. garlic powder
- kosher salt
- Freshly ground black pepper
- 1/4 c. marinara sauce
- 1/4 c. pepperoni
- Fresh basil, for serving

Instructions

Preheat oven to 425º F.

Pulse your steamed broccoli in a food processor until it has a grated-like texture. use a cheesecloth or dish towel and squeeze out the water.

In a big mixing bowl add the broccoli, egg, half of the parmesan and half of the mozzarella and sprinkle with powdered garlic. Season with salt and pepper.

Spray a baking sheet lightly with a cooking oil of your choosing, we recommend olive oil. or use parchment paper. Add your dough and spread it out into a thin crust. Bake the dough until dry, it should take around 15-20 minutes.

Top the broccoli crust with marinara sauce, rest of the cheese and pepperoni. Bake the pizza for another 10 minutes or until crispy. Take it out and spread basil all over the pizza.

The Fake Italian

Ingredients

- 2 whole spaghetti squash
- kosher salt
- Freshly ground black pepper
- Extra-virgin olive oil, for drizzling
- 1 c. chopped pepperoni
- 2 c. marinara
- 2 c. shredded mozzarella
- 1/4 c. chopped parsley

Instructions

Preheat oven to 400º.

Microwave the spaghetti squash for 5 minutes. Slice it in half lengthwise and deseed. Place the two halfs on parchment lined baking sheet, drizzle with olive oil and season with salt and pepper.

Bake, pulp-side down, for around 30 minutes.

Heat a small skillet over medium heat, crisp up pepperoni and transfer to a plate, set aside.

Dig out the pulp using a fork, it should result in spaghetti like strings. Add ¼ cup of mozzarella, ¼ cup of pepperoni and ½ cup of marinara sauce to each half of the squash. Stir the filling with a fork, little by little adding mozzarella and parsley. Transfer the squash back to the baking sheet.

Use the broiling setting to melt the cheese.

Serve immediately!

The Pinwheels

Ingredients

- 1/4 c. marinara
- 1 tsp. dried oregano
- All-purpose flour, for rolling
- 1 Large ball pizza dough
- 8 oz. low-moisture mozzarella, sliced
- 8 oz. thinly sliced pepperoni

Instructions

Preheat oven to 500°.

Place a parchment lined baking sheet in the oven.

Combine marinara sauce and oregano in a small mixing bowl and set aside.

Flour your kitchen counter and roll out the pizza dough and separate it to four equally sized rectangles. Dust the dough with a little flour if needed.

Spoon out thin layer of pizza sauce, leaving a nice sized border for the crust. Do the same with a mozzarella. Roll the border tight into a snail like shape, remove the excess flour with a brush. Place on a sheet pan, with the seams facing down.

Bake for 10 to 15 minutes.

The Pizzadillas

Ingredients

- 1 tbsp. extra-virgin olive oil
- 2 medium flour tortillas
- 1/3 c. pizza sauce
- 1/3 c. pepperoni
- 1 c. shredded mozzarella
- 1/2 c. finely grated Parmesan
- 2 cloves garlic, minced
- Fresh italian parsley, chopped (for garnish)

Instructions

Preheat a medium sized skillet over medium heat and warm up olive oil. Place a tortilla in the skillet and spread half of the pizza sauce on top of the tortilla. Drizzle you cheese over it.

Sprinkle garlic and italian seasoning over the cheese. Scatter pepperoni before topping it off with a second tortilla. Cook until the tortilla is golden.

Preheat broiler.

When the pizzadilla is ready to be flipped, cover the skillet with a large plate. Flip the skillet up-side down and transfer the pizzadilla to the plate. Slide it back onto the skillet again, top with the last pizza sauce, pepperoni, cheese and seasoning.

Put the skillet in the oven and let the cheese melt.

The Time Garlic Bread Met Pizza

Ingredients

- 2 c. shredded mozzarella, divided
- 8 oz. cream cheese, softened
- 1/2 c. ricotta
- 1/4 c. plus 1 tbsp. freshly grated Parmesan, divided
- 1 tbsp. Italian seasoning
- 1/2 tsp. crushed red pepper flakes
- kosher salt
- 1 can refrigerated biscuits
- 2 tbsp. extra-virgin olive oil
- 3 cloves garlic, minced
- 1 tbsp. Freshly Chopped Parsley
- 1/4 c. pizza sauce or marinara
- 1/4 c. mini pepperoni

Instructions

Preheat oven to 350°.

Combine 1¼ cup mozzarella, softened cream cheese, ricotta, ¼ cup Parmesan, Italian seasoning, and red pepper. This is our dip

Cut the biscuits in half and roll into balls. In a large skillet, place the biscuit balls in a circle.
Combine garlic, olive oil and parsley in a mixing bowl. Brush the biscuits with the mixture.

Pour the dip into the middle of the dough circle and spread out some marinara. Top with the rest of the mozzarella, parmesan and pepperoni. Place dip inside of ring and spoon over marinara.

Put the skillet in the oven and let it cook the biscuits through, make sure the cheese is melted!

The Skillet

Ingredients

- 1 tsp. extra-virgin olive oil, plus more for brushing
- 2 Italian sausage links, casings removed
- All-purpose flour, for work surface
- 1 lb. pizza dough, at room temperature
- 1/4 c. pizza sauce
- 1 c. shredded mozzarella
- 1/4 c. sliced pepperoni
- 1 green bell pepper, sliced
- 1/4 small red onion, thinly sliced
- 1/4 c. sliced mushrooms
- 2 tbsp. sliced black olives
- kosher salt
- Freshly ground black pepper

Instructions

Heat oven to 525°.

Preheat a medium sized skillet over medium heat and warm up olive oil. Cook the sausage, break up the sausage, until golden.

Spray a large skillet with a cooking oil of your choosing.

Flour your kitchen counter and roll out the pizza dough until it is the size of your skillet and transfer it to the skillet.

Spoon out the pizza sauce leaving a nice sized edge for the crust. Add the sausage and the rest of the ingredients, season with salt and pepper.

Brush the crust with a generous amount of olive oil and sprinkle with it salt.

Place the skillet in the oven and let it cook the pizza for about 20 to 25 minutes.

The Hot Pocket

Ingredients

- 1 lb. store-bought or homemade pie crust
- 1/2 c. marinara
- 1 1/2 c. shredded mozzarella
- 1/2 c. mini pepperoni
- 1 large egg, beaten with 1 tbsp. water

Instructions

Preheat oven to 350º F

Spray a baking sheet lightly with a cooking oil of your choosing, we recommend olive oil. or use parchment paper.

Flour your kitchen counter and roll out the pie dough and separate it to a rectangle. Slice into four strips.

Spread marinara sauce on one half the strips lengthwise. Sprinkle with mozzarella and top with pepperoni. Fold over tops.

Seal the edges together. Using the egg wash, brush the outside of the hot pockets and place them on the baking sheet/parchment paper.

Bake until golden, 20 minutes.

The Ranch Pig

Ingredients

- 1 tbsp. unsalted butter
- 1 tbsp. all-purpose flour
- 1 c. whole milk
- 2 tbsp. Powdered dip mix
- kosher salt
- Freshly ground black pepper
- 5 tbsp. extra-virgin olive oil, plus more for baking sheet
- 8 oz. pizza dough, at room temperature
- 4 oz. sharp white cheddar, grated
- 4 oz. thinly sliced prosciutto
- Fresh basil, for serving

Instructions

Preheat oven to 450º F.

Heat a small saucepan over medium heat.

Melt butter in the pan. Using a whisk, add in flour and cook, continuously whisking until combined. Mix in milk and boil. Reduce to a simmer, whisk occasionally. Let the mixture thicken up until it gets a heavy cream like consistency. Whisk in powdered dip mix and season with salt and pepper. Let the dip mixture cool off.

Place the oven rack in the bottom of the oven. Line a baking sheet, rim and all, with parchment paper and spray with cooking oil.

Roll out the dough into the baking sheet and set aside.

Pour the dip mixture over the dough and spread cheese topped with prosciutto over the pizza.

Bake the pizza for 10 to 15 minutes.

Season with the basil leaves and pepper.

Ready to serve!

The Swiss

Ingredients

- 2 tbsp. extra-virgin olive oil
- 2 Italian sausages, casings removed
- 2 garlic cloves, minced
- 2 bunches Swiss chard, chopped
- kosher salt
- Freshly ground black pepper
- 1/4 c. cornmeal
- 1 ball fresh pizza dough (if frozen, make sure it's thawed)
- 4 oz. fresh mozzarella, thinly sliced
- 1/2 c. freshly grated Parmesan
- 1/2 to 1 tsp. Crushed red pepper flakes, for garnish

Instructions

Preheat oven to 450º F

Spray a baking sheet lightly with a cooking oil of your choosing, we recommend olive oil. or use parchment paper.

Preheat a medium sized skillet over medium heat and warm up olive oil. Cook the sausage, break up the sausage, until golden. Transfer to a paper lined plate.

Cook garlic for 1 minute in a pan over medium-high heat. Add Swiss chard in two separate batches and stir it for around 5 minutes until wilted. Season with salt and pepper, then using a colander drain the mixture.

Drizzle cornmeal on your kitchen counter and roll out the dough into a big rectangle and place it into a greased baking sheet. Add the remaining mozzarella, sausage and chard, top with parmesan.

Bake pizza for 15 minutes. Spread red pepper, season with salt and black pepper.

The Roll Out

Ingredients

- 1 tube refrigerated pizza dough
- 1 c. pizza or marinara sauce
- 1/2 c. mini pepperoni
- 1 tsp. dried oregano
- 2 c. shredded mozzarella
- 1/2 c. finely grated Parmesan
- 1 pinch red pepper flakes

Instructions

Preheat oven to 375° F

Spray a baking sheet lightly with a cooking oil of your choosing, we recommend olive oil. or use parchment paper.

Roll out the dough into a big rectangle and cut it into 4 equally sized smaller rectangles. Spoon a layer of pizza sauce leaving a nice sized edge for crust. Drizzle with the cheeses, oregano, salt and pepper. Top with pepperoni.

Tightly roll up the dough and seal the edges..

Bake 20 minutes or until the dough gets a nice golden brown color.

Serve warm!

The Pull-Apart Pizza

Ingredients

- 1 roll Pillsbury pizza crust
- 1/4 c. pizza sauce
- 4 cloves garlic, minced
- 1 1/2 c. shredded mozzarella
- 1/2 c. grated Parmesan
- 1/2 c. sliced pepperoni
- 1/2 tsp. dried oregano

Instructions

Preheat oven to 400º F.

Flour your kitchen counter and roll out the dough.

Spoon a layer of pizza sauce and top with garlic.

Slice the dough into a square.

Sprinkle the cheese over the pizza.

Top the cheese with pepperoni.

Cut up the pizza into smaller squares and stack them on top of each other.

Greased a loaf pan and lay down the stacked pizza in it.

Bake until pizza for 25-30 minutes.

Can I Ask For A Favor?

I hope you have enjoyed these recipes and given them a try! If so, then I'd really appreciate it if you would take a couple of minutes of your time and post a short review on Amazon.

I would love to read your comments and recommendations.

Please post your review on Amazon

Thanks for your support!

Happy Cooking!

- Michael Thomsen

Made in the USA
San Bernardino, CA
12 December 2018